Introduction

Hampshire has had a long-held association with railways since 1840, when the first line was built from Southampton to London, followed by many other routes and branches in subsequent decades, some of which have since fallen victim to closure. Nevertheless, there is still a wealth of variety throughout the county, and this book is an illustration of how the railway operated from the end of the twentieth century to the current scene. From a passenger perspective, the primary route has always been the South West Main Line, which bisects the county on its way from Weymouth to London. This line has been in the hands of electric multiple units since the demise of steam in 1967, and the so-called 'slam door' units were the mainstay of the line from that time until the introduction of the immensely popular 'Wessex Electric' Class 442s in 1988, which held sway for almost two decades and were the flagship of the Network South East fleet. By 2005, however, the wholesale introduction of German- and Austrian-built Desiro stock saw the end of the slam-door trains, apart from two units retained for use on the Lymington–Brockenhurst line, but they too were withdrawn in 2009. The Desiro stock brought new levels of comfort for passengers and staff alike, and can be found on all electrified routes in Hampshire, including the main line from Portsmouth to London, which cuts through the eastern edge of the county via the South Downs.

The two main lines to London are linked by the Solent line, which meanders somewhat slowly between the two large South Coast cities of Portsmouth and Southampton, and by a shorter line from Fareham to Eastleigh that provides a second route from Portsmouth to London. In addition to South West Trains, which is the dominant operator in the area, there are also electric trains running along the coast to Sussex and Gatwick provided by Southern Railway and operated by British-built Electrostar units. Alongside these are some 1970s-built Class 313s, which ply the line to Brighton from Portsmouth. In the north of the county is the Basingstoke–Farnborough stretch of track, which has been the scene of high-speed testing in the past. Today it is home to electric commuter services to London, plus the diesel services that have come from Salisbury and the West Country. Just to the west of Basingstoke is Worting Junction, which is where the West of England routes splits from the Weymouth line, but it's a purely diesel route and was home to the Class 50s and then Class 47s in the early 1990s when new diesel multiple units took over the service. Other passenger services run on the branch line to Alton from London, which is where the line transfers to the ownership of the Watercress Line and continues to Alresford on the formation of the line that used to run directly to Winchester. Basingstoke also provides the sight of both prototype Class 150 'Sprinters', operated by Great Western Railway on the shuttle service to Reading, and further east the North Downs Line also briefly interjects into Hampshire on its way between Reading and Gatwick. Diesel services also operate the 'Salisbury Six' route, which provides the Southampton area with an effective local service by running from Salisbury to Romsey via the newest station in the county at Chandlers Ford. The remaining passenger operator is CrossCountry, which used Class 47s and HSTs for many years on the long-distance routes from Bournemouth to the north of England and Scotland, but these were swept away in 2002 by the arrival of Belgian-built Voyager diesel trains. This coincided with the removal of the CrossCountry services that had been running north from Portsmouth via Guildford.

The port of Southampton provides the county with the majority of the freight services that operate alongside the passenger operations. Container traffic has run from Southampton for many decades, and under British Rail they were securely in the hands of Class 47s, which continued after privatisation despite a brief spell of Class 37 traction. Eventually, the Class 47s were replaced by Class 57s, followed by Class 66s and now additionally Class 70s. The Freightliner network from Southampton is not as diverse as it once was, but the port on which the railway thrives is continuing to grow. Almost all Freightliner services head north via Eastleigh, which is where the driver depot is located. This has resulted in the stabling point next to the station historically being host to Type Four traction resting between duties, although these days locomotives are fuelled and watered at Redbridge depot. Eastleigh is still very much the centre of freight activity in the county, and in years gone by the large marshalling yard was regularly full of a huge variety of traffic: from gas tankers, to wagons full of Ford Transits from the Ford plant at Swaythling. These days the yard is more associated with engineering trains operating to various weekend and overnight work sites from the virtual quarry next to the station. Motive power to and from Eastleigh is dominated by GB Railfreight and their fleet of Class 66s and Class 73s, the latter of which have always been at home at Eastleigh. Also present is the colourful Colas Rail and their Class 70s and Class 66s that operate civil engineers' services from the yard; Colas Rail provide a couple of booked trains each day to and from Hoo Junction in Kent. Meanwhile, DB Schenker, the UK's largest freight operator, maintains a large presence in the area operating local freight workings and stone trains to and from

HAMPSHIRE TRACTION

Matthew Taylor

AMBERLEY

First published 2016

Amberley Publishing
The Hill, Stroud
Gloucestershire, GL5 4EP

www.amberley-books.com

ISBN 978 1 4456 6160 5 (print)
ISBN 978 1 4456 6161 2 (ebook)

British Library Cataloguing in Publication Data.
A catalogue record for this book is available from
the British Library.

Typesetting by Amberley Publishing.
Printed in the UK.

the quarry at Merehead in Wiltshire. The oil terminal at Micheldever is just one of many locations that have lost their freight services over the years; a brief attempt was made at a freight terminal at Fratton, but it lasted only weeks in 2009.

Another location that disappeared was the freight yard at Northam in Southampton, which fell into disuse but was reborn in 2004 as the main depot for servicing the Desiro units being delivered for South West Trains at the time, and it is now the largest EMU depot in the county. The only other depot is at Fratton in Portsmouth, which provides some servicing to units heading out on the routes to London via Guildford and Eastleigh. Sidings are provided at Basingstoke and Portsmouth & Southsea, but the large EMU depot that used to be at Eastleigh was closed in the 1990s with work transferring mostly to Fratton. Eastleigh is the location of the works that have been the crucible of railway operations in the county since 1891. Many EMUs were built there, and latterly many locomotives met their end there, with some Class 58s being the most recent examples. The complex of sheds fell into a decline in the 1990s, and closed completely for a brief period at the turn of the century, but is now thriving again with regular visits by local traction and the odd appearance from more unusual locomotive types. Adjacent to the works is the diesel depot, which services visiting DB Schenker locomotives and is home to some rakes of coaches used on weekend charters across the country.

My interest in railways has been there since I was first taken to watch trains at St Cross in Winchester, and is something that I was able to forge into a career, having now spent over twenty years working on the operational railway, mostly in Portsmouth. After progressing from an instant camera to an SLR in 1990, I then made the switch to digital in 2003, but I fortunately had the foresight to retain all the negatives from my film days, with many of those images illustrated in this book. When my interest in trains became apparent, the railway network was full of corporate blue and grey and, although many enthusiasts hanker for the old days when at least in freight terms there was much more variety to be seen, it must be remembered that those days saw all locomotives in the same livery and almost all units in a similarly ubiquitous colour scheme. Fortunately, the 1980s came along and a little bit of colour began to appear, and the eventual appearance of the bright Network South East livery started to make things more interesting. A few years later, along came privatisation, and what followed was a huge number of new liveries bringing a fresh kind of variety to the railway, with every company having its own livery. Apart from the Class 73s, almost nothing still remains from my early days of watching trains, and it is constant change that keeps the railway interesting today and into the future. For the photographer and observer there is still a huge amount to see, and even though some of the more well-established photographic locations are gradually becoming overgrown and hard to use, there are always new spots opening up from time to time to provide a new perspective on familiar subjects.

No. 66420 was one of thirty-four Class 66s delivered for Direct Rail Services, but has since moved to Freightliner after DRS decided to reduce its fleet. Being a more recent addition to the fleet means it gained the updated livery; it is seen here on 13 April 2016 at Worting Junction with 4O51 from Wentloog to Southampton.

Virgin Trains took over the InterCity CrossCountry operation in January 1997, bringing with it the now-commonplace Virgin red livery, which came in a number of slight variations. No. 43008 is seen here partnering No. 43194 on departure from Southampton Central on 22 July 2000 as the 1O11 06.20 Edinburgh–Bournemouth, with mixed liveries in the rake of coaches.

No. 450001 rests under the lights in the Down carriage sidings at Portsmouth & Southsea on 16 May 2013. Southsea usually berths six trains overnight for the following morning, with three being in the carriage sidings. Unfortunately units in these sidings are somewhat exposed and have sometimes been the targets of local graffiti artists.

Class 421 No. 1733 approaches Southampton Central with the 1H23 14.50 Bournemouth–London Victoria on 22 July 2000. In 2002 the Bournemouth services operated by Connex were truncated at Southampton due to growing pathing problems through the New Forest after an increase in services by South West Trains.

Slam-door Class 421 unit No. 1316 keeps company with No. 158818 on 30 April 1993 at Portsmouth Harbour, with the 'Sprinter' occupying platform two, which was permanently taken out of use a few months later. The station at this time was in full Network South East colours, and privatisation was still a year away.

The palindromic No. 220022 passes Battledown flyover and heads south at speed on 13 April 2016 with 1O86 09.35 Newcastle–Southampton. CrossCountry added some new trains to its network recently by extending to Southampton some services that normally terminate at Reading. The new services also created fresh through journeys to Yorkshire and the North East from the South.

Class 67s initially appeared on British shores in late 1999 and were primarily used on Royal Mail services, which only lasted for another four years. Since then they have found frequent use on passenger services with Chiltern Railway, Scotrail, Arriva Trains and on charters. No. 67008 is seen passing Portchester with a rake of VSOE stock on 21 September 2009.

No. 66021 approaching the footbridge at Worting Junction near Basingstoke with 4O39 09.43 Morris Cowley–Southampton Eastern Docks on 13 April 2016. This train is the longest freight service to run on this route and is limited by the capacity of Wallers Ash loop, which is about 10 miles to the south of this popular location.

No. 313201 makes its way between Portsmouth & Southsea and Fratton with 2N26 15.29 Portsmouth Harbour–Brighton on 22 May 2014. Class 313s were introduced in 1976, built as a development of the Class 445 prototype PEP units constructed in the early 1970s; they were the first trains in the UK to be built with the now standard tightlock coupling system.

British Rail often used withdrawn stock for leaf clearing and de-icing duties, and this practice continued in the early years of privatisation. De-icing unit No. 930005 is pictured approaching Southampton on 1 February 2001 in Railtrack livery. This unit is former Class 405 unit No. 4121, dating from 1946.

Class 421 No. 1307 approaches Eastleigh on 20 January 2001 with 1B17 10.15 London Waterloo–Southampton Central. This unit was one of the second batch and was delivered in 1970 to the South West Division for use on Portsmouth line services, replacing Class 404 4-COR units that had been in service since the Portsmouth line was electrified in 1937.

Un-refurbished Class 423 unit No. 3157 leaves Portsea Island and is about to pass under the A27 on 8 May 1993 with the 10.25 Portsmouth Harbour–Wareham. This was a service that called at all stations and had long waits at Southampton and Brockenhurst for faster trains to overtake.

Eastleigh is very much the heart of the railway in Hampshire with a large freight yard at its north end. To the south is the traction depot, the railway works, plus a locomotive stabling point adjacent to the station. Class 423 No. 3576 is pictured on 7 May 2000 with the 15.17 Basingstoke–Brighton.

No. 377134 on 1C41 11.12 Portsmouth Harbour–London Victoria passing over the level crossing at Bedhampton station on 31 March 2016. As with most level crossings, there used to be a signal box monitoring it, which was located on the spot where the grey electrical control cabin can be seen.

No. 158884 is pictured at Eastleigh station on 5 June 2013 with 2R30 08.50 Salisbury–Romsey. The main station building has remained largely unchanged since it was built, but the original platform one was removed in the mid-1980s in a cost-cutting measure, with the main station building having previously been located on an island platform.

No. 377150 crosses the bridge over the River Itchen as it approaches Bitterne station on 1C69 14.11 Southampton Central–London Victoria on 10 October 2013. Class 377 is now possibly the largest class on the UK network, with well over 200 examples in service across the Southern and Thameslink networks.

Class 442 No. 2421 is pictured at rest in platform three at Portsmouth Harbour station on 30 April 1993 with the 15.06 to London Waterloo via Guildford. These 'Wessex Electric' units were the last vehicles to be built for the British market to retain first-class compartments, although they were removed when the units moved to Gatwick Express.

No. 170305 is pictured running non-stop through Cosham with No. 170303 on 1O31 10.08 Reading–Brighton on 26 January 2001. Despite being generally popular with train crew and passengers, the Class 170s left South West Trains in 2007 in return for eight Class 158s from TransPennine, which were refurbished and became three-car Class 159s.

Class 59s were in many ways pioneers for the ubiquitous Class 66 that appeared a decade or so later. Nos 59101–59104 were initially owned by Amey Roadstone and worked out of Merehead Quarry, which continued after transfer to EWS in 1998. No. 59101 is seen here passing the A27 near Havant with 7V07 12.40 Chichester–Merehead on 7 October 2010.

No. 450021 is pictured leaving Farnborough with 2B36 09.50 Poole–London Waterloo on 18 March 2016. Opened in 1838, the original station had an island platform in the middle that was removed when the line was quadrupled. It is sometimes known as Farnborough Main to differentiate it from the nearby Farnborough North station.

At the open day at Eastleigh Works on 6 May 1990, the latest of the initial batch of sixteen refurbished Class 421 units was on display, and it provided a first sight of the experimental marker lights on unit No. 1315. No further units had these lights fitted and, in later years, No. 1315 had the light panels plated over.

Despite the short load on 1 May 1997, a pair of Class 47s in the form of Nos 47225 and 47301 were provided for 4O25 13.34 Ripple Lane–Southampton Container Terminal. Both locomotives display the recently applied Freightliner branding near the cab doors. Class 47s were by this time in their final years on these services.

The small Freightliner maintenance depot at Redbridge near Southampton, which serves the adjacent container terminal, is usually home to one or two Class 08 shunters in addition to Class 66s and Class 70s receiving fuel or light repairs. No. 08785 soaks up the spring sunshine with No. 66532 for company on 8 April 2014.

No. 444021 arrives into Portsmouth & Southsea station on 16 April 2010 with 1P32 10.15 Portsmouth Harbour–London Waterloo. At roughly this point, a spur used to branch off to the right and follow what is now Stanhope Road towards the Royal Navy dockyard; it was still in use as recently as 1977 but was removed soon after.

No. 221126 departs from Southampton Central on 6 April 2013 with 1M42 10.45 Bournemouth–Manchester Piccadilly. In years gone by, the CrossCountry network from Poole and Bournemouth was far more diverse, with services to Scotland via both east and west coast routes, but rationalisation in 2003 saw Manchester become the sole destination from Bournemouth.

Southampton Parkway station has seen great change in recent years, with new station buildings, waiting shelters, a multi-storey car park and a new footbridge, plus a slight name change. Class 423 unit No. 3432 is pictured calling at platform one with a London Waterloo service on 4 November 1991 in a fresh coat of Network South East livery.

Above: No. 158955 arrives at Cosham on 21 October 2014 with 1F07 08.30 Cardiff–Portsmouth just as No. 377463 departs with 1N65 10.33 Brighton–Southampton. Despite substantial growth in passenger numbers, there has been very little change on the Portsmouth–Cardiff route, which remains just an hourly service of three coaches.

Below: Class 422 unit No. 2256 is seen resting at Fratton depot on 13 March 1999. It was delivered in 1970 and spent most of its life working from London Victoria, but was transferred to South West Trains in 1997. In 1999, it had its buffet car removed to make it a standard Class 421, which is how it stayed until withdrawal in 2004.

Colas Rail is a fairly new player in the UK rail market, having commenced operations in 2007 using a small fleet of Class 47s. Colas has since expanded and ordered new Class 70s, in addition to taking five Class 66s from Freightliner. No. 66846 awaits its next turn of duty at Eastleigh on 11 May 2015.

Class 411 No. 1539 waits at a red signal just ahead of Portcreek Junction with 2T31 11.40 London Waterloo–Portsmouth Harbour via Eastleigh on 24 August 2000. The 1980s saw the development of the industrial estate in the background, which had previously been derelict land, surrounded on all three sides by railway lines.

Shortly before loco-hauled stock was replaced by more modern stock, a number of Class 47/7s were added to the fleet to improve reliability. No. 47747 is looking smart in preparation for a naming ceremony at Poole station just a few days later, and is seen here at Southampton with 1O09 08.17 Manchester–Bournemouth on 17 August 2000.

No. 450024 calls at Bedhampton station with 2P38 11.24 Portsmouth & Southsea to London Waterloo on 31 March 2016. Although the line to Portsmouth was opened in 1848, Bedhampton station didn't open until 1906. Nowadays it only sees two trains per hour in each direction, as most people use nearby Havant station.

In 1997 Connex South Central created eleven three-car Class 421/7s by reforming some withdrawn Class 422 units with the buffet cars and compartments removed. They were used on services along the coast between Brighton, Portsmouth Harbour and Eastbourne. No. 1408 is seen passing Hilsea on 12 November 1999 with the 10.30 Brighton–Portsmouth Harbour.

No. 66127 is seen heading south past Bevois Park sidings in Southampton with an engineers' working from Eastleigh Yard on 10 October 2013, while Class 377 unit No. 377429 prepares to stop at a signal for the Class 66 to pass through the narrow twin-track section in Southampton tunnel.

No. 444028 approaches the quiet station of Bedhampton on 31 March 2016 with 1P38 11.45 Portsmouth Harbour–Waterloo. Class 444s are now the primary mainline unit type, having displaced Classes 421 and 442, although they worked alongside the Wessex Electrics for a couple of years after their introduction in 2004.

The InterCity 125 revitalised the long-distance network in the 1970s and 1980s; the fact that it is still in frontline service in many parts of the country forty years after it was first introduced in 1976 is a testament to the design. No. 43029 is seen approaching Southampton Central on 15 January 2000 with the 11.20 Bournemouth–Edinburgh.

No. 377328 is seen passing Hilsea on 8 January 2010 with 2S62 11.59 Portsmouth & Southsea–Littlehampton. Class 377/3 units were built as Class 375/3 but were very swiftly reclassified when they had their coupling mechanism changed in 2003. They are now concentrated on South London routes, following the arrival of Class 313s in 2010.

No. 159015 leads Nos 159013 and 159005 in from the west and on to the third-rail-powered South West Main Line at Worting Junction on 13 April 2016 with 1L32 08.23 from Exeter and 1O32 08.50 from Bristol. These services combine at Salisbury with an additional three coaches from the depot, forming a nine-car service to London Waterloo.

Above: Class 442 No. 2407 is at Eastleigh with a service to Poole on 2 April 1989. This particular unit suffered damage on 3 September 1989 after running away through the buffer stops in Bournemouth depot, with half of the unit ending up on a main road. Fortunately, it happened at night so there were no injuries.

Below: Class 421 No. 1905 arrives at Southampton on 7 April 2000 with the 12.50 Bournemouth–London Victoria via Hove. This was another of the original 'Phase 1' units delivered in 1963 for services from London Victoria; it was renumbered 1728 following refurbishment in the 1980s before joining the Class 421/9 sub-class some years later as 1905.

Class 423 units began to appear in the late 1960s and were refurbished in the late 1980s, with additional seating created by reducing the size of the guard's van. Withdrawals began in 2004 and, by the end of 2005, they had all been retired. No. 3482 heads out of Eastleigh depot on 4 March 1990.

In 1998 a number of redundant Class 47s found new life as Class 57s initially for use with Freightliner. No. 57005 was one of the first batch of six locomotives and had previously spent a considerable time dumped at Crewe as No. 47350. It is seen here on 17 August 2000 approaching Southampton Central with 4E74 12.30 Southampton–Leeds.

No. 158884 sits in the reception road at Fratton depot on 8 January 2010, following heavy snowfalls two days previously. Despite it being a weekday, the inclement weather had resulted in fewer trains running than usual, so this unit spent the day resting in the cold awaiting a call to duty the following morning.

Nine-car mixed formations of Class 450 and Class 444 stock are not common, but it does happen sometimes when a depot is short of a unit. Nos 450071 and 444003 are pictured at Worting Junction on 13 April 2016 with 2B32 08.50 Poole–London Waterloo, which is usually just a single Class 450 unit.

No. 66230 was one of the last of the EWS Class 66 locomotives to arrive in the UK in April 2000, just nineteen months after the first boat load of locomotives docked in Newport. It is seen here shortly after leaving Southampton Western Docks with a trip working to Eastleigh Yard on 18 April 2013.

Class 455s are the workhorse of the suburban network on South West Trains; on 19 May 2016, No. 5739 is pictured approaching Southampton Central with 5Y51 14.32 Bournemouth Depot–Wimbledon Park stock movement. This is one of forty-three 455/7 units built in 1985 with the addition of a trailer from a Class 508, which is easily identified by its lower roof profile.

Nos 221115 and 221105 are pictured passing Eastleigh on 7 May 2002 with 1O38 09.10 Edinburgh–Bournemouth. Both units are only a few weeks old and have yet to have their additional trailers added to make them into their correct five-car formations. Paired units were not that uncommon in the early days of Voyager operation.

On 17 August 2000, No. 2304 approaches Southampton with 1B28 11.00 Poole–London Waterloo. Class 412 units were essentially a Class 411 with a buffet car, and were mostly used on the route between Portsmouth and Waterloo in combination with Class 421 units. Like most Mk 1 stock, they were withdrawn in 2005 when Class 450 units were delivered.

In the 1980s the 73/2 sub-class was created to provide a pool of locomotives for Gatwick Express services. The twelve locomotives were all painted in InterCity livery, which has been recreated in this view of No. 73205 at Eastleigh on 10 October 2013. By this time No. 73205 was part of the GB Railfreight fleet and was a regular visitor to Eastleigh.

In October 1987 a new corporate identity was revealed for the freight sectors of British Rail, which consisted of a two-tone grey livery with decals denoting the business sector to which the locomotive was allocated. No. 47051 is seen here running light through Southampton Central on 4 November 1991, wearing the red-and-yellow diamond Railfreight Distribution logo.

No. 70009 is pictured in Millbrook container terminal with a Freightliner service to the north on 18 April 2013. This terminal is purely for transfer of containers to road transport, while the main container terminal is a mile to the west and serves some of the largest ships that sail on the world's oceans.

Consecutively numbered units pass each other at Fratton on 21 March 2015 with No. 450040 handling the rear of 1P15 07.30 London Waterloo–Portsmouth Harbour while No. 450041 is at the rear of 5P30 08.58 Fratton Depot–Portsmouth Harbour empty stock, which will then form the 09.45 to London.

Class 423 No. 3469 goes for a wash in the elderly washing plant at Fratton depot on 13 March 1999, which was replaced soon afterwards in preparation for the arrival of new Siemens Desiro stock. Class 423s were introduced across the south in 1967 to replace stock that had displaced steam power some thirty years earlier.

No. 58030 is seen here running light through Eastleigh station on 26 January 2001 in fairly grim conditions, indicative of the future of the Class 58s, which was bleak at best in 2001 with the class being entirely withdrawn less than two years later. This locomotive was one of many that found further work in Spain where it remains today.

Looking south from the bridge at the end of Eastleigh station provides this view across the stabling point, which, on 10 September 2010, was quite full with a former DRS Class 66 and six GB Railfreight Class 73s. Nearest is No. 73207 in large logo livery, which was carried by a small number of the class in their BR days.

Class 66s working in tandem are not uncommon by any means and it's often an easy way of moving a locomotive to a specific location for repairs or servicing. No. 66581 leads No. 66517 down the gradient from Battledown flyover near Basingstoke on 13 April 2016 with 6M66 09.32 Southampton–Garston in Merseyside.

On a wet 23 April 1994 Class 421 No. 1831 approaches Hilsea on the 08.25 Brighton–Portsmouth Harbour, having called at all stations and taking almost an hour and a half for the 45-mile journey. Despite it being a Saturday, the car park appears to be full of a selection of cars typical of the era.

After fifty years working on the London Underground, ten Class 483 units were created at Eastleigh from former 1938 stock. After conversion and testing, they were sent to the Isle of Wight where they are now the oldest stock in regular use on the national network. No. 008 is pictured at Eastleigh on 6 May 1990 after conversion.

No. 377445 prepares to stop at Portchester on 22 September 2009 with 1C37 10.11 Southampton–London Victoria as No. 377109 rounds the corner towards Fareham with 1J54 08.32 Victoria–Southampton. Nestled on the lower slope of Portsdown Hill, Portchester has only recently seen the benefit of frequent services to Victoria.

No. 158837 leaves Southampton on 19 May 2001 with 1V94 09.00 Brighton–Bristol Temple Meads in original Regional Railways livery. The two daily Bristol–Brighton services have been running for decades and have survived a number of timetable rewrites to provide a convenient direct link for those in Sussex heading west.

No. 450074 heads north on 10 October 2013 past the River Itchen before crossing St Denys Junction and heading off to Portsmouth & Southsea. Adjacent to this spot is Bevois Park sidings, which were out of use for a number of years, but have recently come back in to service for aggregate services provided by DB Schenker.

On 17 March 2010, No. 37610 passes under Fratton Bridge with a test train operated on behalf of Network Rail. No. 37610 was by this time in its fourth incarnation since delivery in 1963, incarnations that included a spell as one of a batch of locomotives provided for the proposed Eurostar overnight services, which never materialised.

Brockenhurst is something of a gateway to the New Forest and forms the start of the line to Lymington Pier, which was the last route in the UK to see slam door EMUs. No. 220006 is seen on 1O06 06.37 Nottingham–Bournemouth, while a northbound Voyager unit passes in the opposite direction on 19 May 2016.

Class 442 No. 2421 leaving Havant on 30 April 1993 with the 15.06 Portsmouth Harbour–London Waterloo. The Class 442s spent nearly twenty years on services from London Waterloo before being displaced by Desiro stock. After a period of storage, they moved to Gatwick Express although they are now facing an uncertain future again.

No. 43068 is seen at Southampton Central on 4 November 1991 with a southbound 'Inter Regional' service from the north of England to Bournemouth. The HSTs had made their debut on cross-country workings through Hampshire only a few months earlier and this particular locomotive was a former ECML example displaced by Class 91s.

No. 66533 is seen emerging from Southampton Tunnel on 19 May 2016 with 4O51 09.56 Wentloog–Southampton. The tunnel continues to have issues with water penetration despite major works in the 1980s and again a few years ago; it has also become a bottleneck in an increasingly busy area of railway operations.

No. 450030 crosses the viaduct over Fareham Creek as it heads east on 1T37 13.09 London Waterloo–Portsmouth Harbour via Eastleigh on 25 June 2014. Since their introduction in 2003, Class 450s have been the backbone of the outer suburban fleet from London Waterloo, although they quite often operate express services.

The Portsmouth–Cardiff route has been in the hands of Class 158 units for many years but they are replaced by Class 150/2 units, should Canton depot in Cardiff be short of serviceable 158s. Prior to their refurbishment, the use of 150s on this route was very unsuitable and on a warm 24 August 2000 I'm sure the allocation of No. 150246 to 1F20 13.24 Portsmouth–Cardiff was unpopular with the passengers.

Towards the end of 2000, South West Trains acquired a fleet of nine brand-new Class 170/3 units, which were used on all of their diesel routes, although they rarely ventured west of Salisbury. No. 170301 is pictured with No. 170303 leaving Winchester on 20 January 2001, with 1V28 11.00 Brighton–Reading.

Class 421 unit No. 1863 wearing Connex South Central livery passes the playing fields of Warblington school as it approaches Havant on 29 May 1999 with the 16.30 Brighton–Portsmouth Harbour. In the late 1980s a refurbishment program saw all Class 421/2 units pass through Eastleigh for cosmetic facelift-ing.

Colas Rail initially operated trains using a small fleet of Class 47 locomotives, which were soon supplemented by Class 56s. They now have ten brand-new Class 70 locomotives with a further seven currently on order. No. 70809 is seen on 18 December 2015 approaching Southampton tunnel, running light engine from Westbury to Eastleigh.

The annual diesel gala at the Swanage Railway in Dorset in recent years has provided the pleasant sight of unusual modern and not-so-modern traction making its way to and from Wareham for the connection to the heritage line. On 14 May 2013, Nos 20227, 20189 and 20142 lead Class 423 unit No. 3417 through a damp Millbrook station.

All Class 60s were delivered in two-tone Railfreight colours with relevant sector decals. Around half a dozen were allocated to Hither Green, becoming quite regular at Eastleigh; No. 60026 from the petroleum sector was one of them. It is seen here leaving Eastleigh with the Hallen Marsh–Furzebrook LPG tanks on 10 May 1991.

Class 204, 205 and 207 units, also known as 'Hampshire Units', were a familiar sight, particularly in South Hampshire from the 1960s until the electrification of lines from Portsmouth to St Denys and Eastleigh in 1990. No. 207017 is seen approaching Eastleigh on 4 March 1990 with what would probably have been a service from Southampton to Reading.

In 2000, Wales & West gained an additional pair of Class 158s from ScotRail after the introduction of Class 170s to Scottish express routes. Both units were soon painted in a new livery to reflect their new roles and No. 158746 is seen here at Cosham on 13 November 2000 with 1F05 07.30 Cardiff–Portsmouth, sporting the new look.

No. 159018 leaving Eastleigh station on 27 January 2001 with 1V32 13.00 Brighton–Reading. The Brighton to Reading or Basingstoke services were a very useful second hourly service over the Eastleigh to Fareham line and, at one time, South West Trains had ambitious plans to extend them to Birmingham using Class 159s, although this never came to fruition.

Class 70 locomotives had a difficult early life, not only with teething problems but also when No. 70012 fell victim to an unloading accident at Newport and was withdrawn before even entering service. Despite ordering thirty locomotives, Freightliner only took delivery of nineteen of the class. No. 70016 is seen at Basingstoke on 4 September 2015 with 4O51 09.58 Wentloog–Southampton.

No. 450098 at the head of 1P23 09.30 London Waterloo–Portsmouth Harbour passing Farlington on 7 October 2010. When the Class 442s were put in store in 2007, many of the Class 444 fleet migrated to the Weymouth line, leaving an increased number of Class 450s on Portsmouth services to the dismay of many passengers.

Class 150 units are the oldest of the second-generation diesel units but are still found in great numbers across the country and First Great Western still has a significant fleet of the units. On 1 November 2014, No. 150238 is seen in the 'Dynamic Lines' livery leading No. 158960 into Fratton station with 1F16 11.23 Portsmouth Harbour–Cardiff Central.

Class 165s were introduced by Network South East in 1991 and were delivered in both two-car and three-car versions. They replaced the venerable Class 207 and Class 205 units that had been operating between Reading and Basingstoke for many years. No. 165118 is seen at Basingstoke on 16 December 2000 with 2J24 11.35 Basingstoke–Reading.

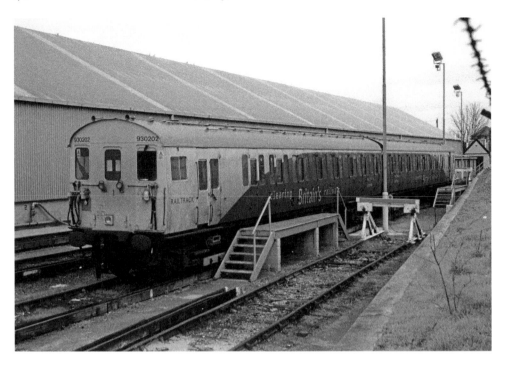

On 7 March 2000, departmental unit No. 930202 is pictured in Railtrack livery at Fratton depot. Units such as these were used for leaf clearing in autumn and de-icing in winter. This is a former Class 416/2 built in 1954 for suburban services from Victoria and London Bridge before being displaced by more modern stock.

The Class 60 fleet was still in widespread use across Britain in 2000, but by 2004 they began accumulating in numbers for storage at Toton depot prior to a resurgence in their use by 2012. No. 60016 is seen here approaching Southampton Central on 7 April 2000 with the weekly 6V99 12.43 Hamworthy–Cardiff Tidal.

On 18 March 2016 Class 455 Nos 5727 and 5905 are pictured leaning into the curve on the approach to Farnborough as they head south for some maintenance at Bournemouth on 5B39 10.01 Wimbledon Park–Bournemouth Depot. Although it's extremely rare, Class 455s have been known to operate in service as far as Basingstoke.

No. 66414 was one of a very small fleet of Freightliner Class 66 locomotives to wear the Stobart livery and had the name *James the Engine*, but it had a rather tatty look to it after the decals were removed. It is seen here on 8 April 2014 at Millbrook with 4O51 09.58 Wentloog–Southampton.

Autumnal colour is vividly on display as No. 450082 approaches Winchfield station on 10 November 2010 with 2L44 13.24 Basingstoke–Waterloo. The route between Woking and Basingstoke was the setting for high-speed test runs of bogies for Eurostar trains in the 1990s with the bogies placed under Class 33 locomotive No. 33115.

No. 1731 at Cosham on 13 May 1991 with a Bournemouth–London Victoria service. This unit entered service in 1964 as No. 7320 and was part of the initial batch of Class 421 units built for mainline services radiating from London Victoria. A repaint into Connex livery followed for this unit for its final years before withdrawal in 2004.

No. 158889 is seen at Redbridge station on 6 May 2013 about to diverge to the right with 2R38 12.07 Romsey–Salisbury. This is one of eleven Class 158 units that moved from ScotRail and TransPennine routes in 2007 in a change that saw all nine Class 170s also move from South West Trains to TransPennine.

The stretch of track from Cosham Junction to Farlington Junction currently only sees one daily service by South West Trains and is mostly used by Southern Rail services heading to and from Southampton, as seen here with No. 377101 just leaving the main line at Farlington on 7 October 2010 with 1N12 10.33 Southampton–Brighton.

Class 442 Wessex Electric unit No. 2404 accelerates away from the speed restriction over Portcreek Bridge on 24 August 2000 as it heads north with 1P40 13.50 Portsmouth Harbour–London Waterloo. These trains were a welcome improvement on slam-door stock when they started to take over the fast services on the Portsmouth line in 1992.

Northam depot in Southampton is the location of Siemens' maintenance facility for Class 444 and Class 450 stock, carrying out almost all work on the units and acting as a berthing point. No. 444015 is pictured here passing the washing plant on 19 May 2016 as it heads out on 5E54 14.56 Northam–Havant.

Seen here leaving Fratton with 2N69 14.57 Littlehampton–Portsmouth & Southsea on 12 March 2014, No. 313202 was one of a batch of units to take over services on the Euston–Watford DC lines in 1985. They were displaced by Class 378s in 2010 but surprisingly further use was found for them and they broke new ground by operating coastal services from Brighton.

In 2000 Anglia launched an innovative new service providing six daily return trips between East Anglia and Basingstoke via Staines, West Hampstead and Stratford. Increasing timetable constraints on the North London Line plus low passenger numbers saw the service withdrawn in September 2002. No. 170203 is pictured at Basingstoke on 16 December 2000 with 1L90 10.31 Basingstoke–Colchester.

In 1999 South West Trains created an additional eight 'Greyhound' Class 421/8 units from redundant Class 422 units, whose buffet cars were removed and replaced with standard coaches from spare Class 411 units. One such unit was No. 1397, which is pictured here approaching Southampton with 1B44 15.10 Poole–London Waterloo on 22 July 2000.

No. 47839 looking smart as it coasts past the marshalling yard at Eastleigh on 20 January 2000 with 1O06 06.17 Manchester–Bournemouth. After release from its duties at Virgin Trains in 2003, No. 47839 went on to spend a decade with Riviera Trains before finally succumbing to the cutter's torch in August 2013 at Eastleigh works.

On a frosty 19 December 1999, Class 421 No. 1736 is seen heading south through Hilsea with the 10.17 London Victoria–Portsmouth Harbour. This was one of a number of slam-door units that were painted in a white livery, which was the final livery to be carried by this unit.

Class 73 locomotives with dual power supply have been a constant feature across southern England since the mid-1960s but since privatisation their geographical scope has included almost the entire national network, even as far as the Scottish Highlands. No. 73128 is seen here in EWS livery with 1Z14 05.49 Stewarts Lane–Woking test train at Eastleigh on 13 March 2001.

No. 450095 at Basingstoke station in the early evening of 9 January 2010 with 2L58 16.54 Basingstoke–London Waterloo. Basingstoke is unusual in that platform one is in the Down direction; it's believed this was the case because the Southern Railway didn't want the Great Western Railway to have the prestige of operating from platform one.

No. 70015 approaching Southampton Central on 6 June 2014 with 4O51 09.58 Wentloog–Southampton Container Terminal. Originally Southampton West, the station was rebuilt in 1967 when the route to Bournemouth was electrified and became Southampton Central, following the closure of Southampton Terminus station.

In the early 1990s the sidings adjacent to Eastleigh station were used to stable locomotives between Freightliner duties, with Class 47s and Class 37s frequently prominent in the years before Class 66s ruled the lines. Nowadays stock is generally stabled at Redbridge near the container terminal. No. 37800 is seen at Eastleigh on 8 May 1994.

This unit was one of two prototypes built in 1984 by BREL, leading to 135 further orders of the type. No. 150001 spent many years working in the Midlands but currently operates for Great Western on Basingstoke–Reading shuttles, and is seen here at Basingstoke on 4 September 2015 on 2J35 13.07 Reading–Basingstoke.

Dating from the 1960s, No. 07007 has been employed almost daily at Eastleigh works since at least the mid-1970s and is pictured on 6 May 2013. At a time when several classmates met their end at that location, this is the one that got away; remarkably, seven of the thirteen Class 07s that were built have made it to preservation.

Class 412 No. 2304, on the 17.07 Havant–Waterloo on 29 May 1999, passes Havant Junction. This was the scene of the 'Battle Of Havant' in 1858, with the London, Brighton & South Coast Railway refusing access to their line through the town for the London & South Western Railway, who wanted to start services to London on their own line via Guildford. After a year, an agreement was reached between the companies.

Since their displacement by Class 33s on Portsmouth–Bristol workings in the early 1980s, Class 31s have not been common in Hampshire other than for a short spell on the evening Brighton service by Wessex Trains in 2004. No. 31190 in original two-tone British Railways Green livery is seen stabled at Eastleigh on 14 May 2014.

No. 66594 waits at the signal protecting Basingstoke Junction with 4O54 06.12 Leeds–Southampton on 18 March 2016. In the background can just be seen the new Network Rail Regional Operations Centre, which already provides much of the signalling in the area and is also used by South West Trains as a staff training academy.

Class 421 No. 1719 looking smart as it approaches Southampton Central in a recently applied coat of Connex livery on 17 August 2000 with 1H11 11.50 Bournemouth–London Victoria. At 131 miles this represented almost the longest route that the Class 421s ever operated; it ran along the coast and then to Victoria via Horsham and Gatwick Airport.

Class 50s were regulars on the Waterloo–Exeter route throughout the 1980s until their replacement by Class 159s in 1993. The class is well represented in preservation but not common on the mainline; however, on 11 June 2016 Nos 50007 and 50050 are seen leading 1Z50 04.48 Derby–Swanage.

Class 423 unit No. 3427 is seen crossing Portcreek on 31 March 1997 with a service from Southampton to Portsmouth Harbour. This was a hybrid unit as the leading coach is from a Class 421, although this was only a temporary measure due to accident damage to the original vehicle. Mixed stock became more commonplace as slam-door trains approached their retirement.

No. 220030 is seen heading north through Eastleigh on 8 April 2014 with 1M42 10.45 Bournemouth–Manchester. Although there was a modest increase in services, the replacement of loco–hauled stock saw mostly seven-coach trains replaced by four- or five-coach trains, which has resulted in frequent overcrowding on this and other CrossCountry routes.

No. 377470 pokes its nose out from under the canopy of Portsmouth & Southsea high level on 16 April 2010 with 1C33 10.12 Portsmouth Harbour–London Victoria. The current station design is from 1988 when the high-level platforms were rebuilt from their dark and dismal previous incarnations.

Built in the 1930s, this Kof II shunter spent most of its career working in Germany but arrived in the UK in 1990 for use on the Channel Tunnel project. It then found work in Hong Kong before returning to the UK, eventually ending up as a shunter around Eastleigh works where it is pictured on 10 October 2013.

1 January 2014 saw No. 450110 arrive severely delayed at Southampton with 2E48 15.42 Portsmouth & Southsea–Southampton Central, having been the victim of an arboreal incursion between Portchester and Fareham after a tree blew onto the line in high winds. Some remains of the tree can still be seen on the damaged coupler in this view.

No. 166201 is seen leaving Farnborough North station with 2V58 10.34 Redhill–Reading on 18 March 2016. The North Downs line services used to continue to Tonbridge in Kent but, after that route was electrified for Eurostar diversionary purposes, the diesel service was diverted to run to Gatwick Airport after a reversal at Redhill.

Class 58s first appeared in 1982 and, in the 1990s, they began to find work in the Home Counties, but by 2002 their time was up. Although some were exported to the Continent, Nos 58002 and 58037 were among a number dumped at Eastleigh prior to scrapping on site shortly after this picture was taken on 6 May 2013.

Class 421 unit No. 1303 leaves Cosham station on 13 November 2000 with the 09.47 Southampton Central–Portsmouth Harbour. On the right in this image is all that is left of the small shunting yard at Cosham, including one shed that remains from those bygone days. A small car park is the sole part of the former yard still in railway use.

Class 411 unit No. 1699 still retains Network South East livery at Winchester with 2T24 10.54 Portsmouth Harbour–London Waterloo via Eastleigh on 16 December 2000. This station was known as Winchester City for a lengthy period until 1967 to distinguish it from Winchester (Chesil), which was served by services from Newbury via Whitchurch, closing in 1961.

In 1998 Portsmouth was connected to the CrossCountry network again with three daily services. Structural limitations at Portsmouth Harbour meant that the services soon had to be curtailed at Portsmouth & Southsea, which is where No. 47814 is seen in this image on 24 October 2000 with 1M32 14.40 Portsmouth & Southsea–Blackpool North.

Despite having a corporate livery of its own, GB Railfreight has a number of Class 73s in different liveries. One of them is No. 73119 in traditional BR Blue, which all class members carried through the 1970s; it is seen here outside the main shed at Eastleigh Works on 10 September 2010.

No. 66561 leads a collection of engineering wagons over Battledown flyover on 13 April 2016 with 6V27 13.28 Eastleigh–Hinksey Yard in Oxford, having run light engine from Didcot earlier in the day. Two fellow railway photographers look on at this popular spot for railway photography a few miles from Basingstoke.

Eastleigh Works has had an association with Class 455s since the first overhauls on the fleet began in the late 1980s, and it continues today, with both South West Trains and Southern fleets being worked on at the site. No. 455834 is seen on 18 April 2013 getting a final touch up prior to departing for Selhurst.

Approaching Southampton Central on 1 February 2001 is Class 442 No. 2409 with 1W08 Weymouth–London Waterloo. The Class 442s retained their Network South East livery until the late 1990s, when they were refurbished in Crewe and received the now standard South West Trains mainline livery until moving to Gatwick Express in 2008.

No. 444016 passes St Denys as it speeds towards its next stop at Southampton Central on 10 October 2013 with 2B35 12.39 London Waterloo–Poole. Although being a fairly fast service as far as Eastleigh, it then takes two hours to cover the remaining 40 miles with lengthy stops at Southampton Central and Brockenhurst.

No. 158956 crawls into Fratton station in crisp autumnal sunshine on 1 November 2014 with 1F07 08.30 Cardiff–Portsmouth. Class 158s have been resident on this line since they were brand new back in 1991 as two car sets; in 2005, Wessex Trains reformed and renumbered them to three-car sets, and this has continued with First Great Western.

In 1994 National Power ordered six Class 59s for use on coal and limestone workings in Yorkshire. In 1998, they were transferred to the EWS fleet but to this day remain in the care of Mendip Rail along with the rest of the Class 59 fleet. No. 59201 is seen here passing Portchester station on the weekly Chichester–Merehead empty working on 21 September 2009.

Class 70 No. 70099 was built in Turkey and was used as a demonstrator locomotive until it was shipped to Britain in 2013. Despite having the base livery of Freightliner, it became part of the Colas Rail fleet as No. 70801 and is pictured here at Redbridge Freightliner depot shortly after arrival in the UK on 5 June 2013.

On 10 October 2013, No. 377403 is seen passing St Denys with 1N18 13.33 Southampton Central–Brighton. Since the removal of services to Bournemouth, Southampton now represents the westernmost point of the Southern Railway network and has since benefited from a doubling of services with the addition of a service to Brighton that had previously run from Portsmouth Harbour.

Seen here on 4S59 15.13 Millbrook–Coatbridge on 22 August 2000, No. 47287 was one of a small number of locomotives that were fitted with multiple working equipment, which can be identified by the jumper cable socket in the former headcode box. The locomotive is wearing the revised Railfreight Distribution livery but minus the branding and depot plaque.

Class 450 No. 450551 on 19 May 2016 with 2E41 14.44 Southampton–Portsmouth & Southsea squeezing its way through the narrow stretch of track between Southampton Central and Northam Junction. This twin-track section is increasingly becoming a bottleneck as both freight and passenger traffic levels increase.

Class 411 unit No. 1566 is pictured on a crisp morning at Cosham on 1 February 2001 with 2E11 08.47 Southampton–Portsmouth Harbour. Headcode 85 was for stopping services along the Solent coast, although route codes are a thing of the past, as they no longer appear in either the timetable or on the trains.

No. 166204 passes through the outskirts of Farnborough on 18 March 2016 with 1V41 10.03 Gatwick Airport–Reading. The unit is wearing the current livery of Great Western Railway, which is still operated by the First Group. The green livery harks back to the days of Isambard Kingdom Brunel and the green of the original Great Western Railway.

No. 159102 dives under Battledown flyover near Basingstoke, taking the non-electrified route to Salisbury and beyond on 13 April 2016 with 1L39 13.50 Waterloo–Yeovil Pen Mill. The unit is wearing a revised version of South West Trains livery, which was only applied to two units before getting a slight modification.

Eastleigh has long been a graveyard for various units, particularly Class 33 locomotives, but in 2013 it also became the place where large numbers of London Underground vehicles were scrapped. Two such coaches are seen on 10 October 2013, having just arrived by road from Acton.

In 1979 several Mk 2 carriages were modified for use on Glasgow–Edinburgh express services but in 1990 they moved south for use on Norwich–London services. They were again displaced in 2005. No. 9701 found further use with Network Rail and is seen here passing Cosham on 25 November 2009 with No. 31465 at the rear, providing the power.

Like several other classmates, No. 73206 spent many years operating the London Victoria–Gatwick Airport shuttles and then passed on to GB Railfreight after Gatwick Express took delivery of Class 460 units. Looking down from the bridge at the end of Eastleigh station enables this view, which also shows No. 73141 with another variation of the GB Railfreight livery on 18 April 2013.

On 3 June 2013 No. 158766 is seen at Portsmouth Harbour with 1F12 09.24 to Cardiff running as a two-car unit instead of the usual three-car Class 158/9. Also visible in this image is the now defunct platform two, which was taken out of use in 1994 due to the structural weakness of the pier under the station.

No. 444015 eases down the gradient from the high-level platforms at Portsmouth & Southsea on 6 June 2016 with 1T54 09.59 Portsmouth Harbour–London Waterloo via Eastleigh. The skyline in this area continues to change and, in the background, the old goods yard plus three of the low-level platforms were lost to retail development many years ago.

Class 377 'Electrostar' No. 377122 is seen arriving at Cosham on 21 October 2014 with 1C53 12.11 Southampton–London Victoria. With ten trains an hour, this level crossing located at the bottom end of Cosham High Street is particularly busy. It lost its signal box in the early 1980s not long after the full automatic crossing barriers appeared.

Class 423 No. 3476 is seen crossing Portcreek with the 08.37 Portsmouth Harbour–Southampton on 11 May 1994. The train has just passed under Hilsea Lines and through what is reputed to be the shortest tunnel on the UK railway. Hilsea Lines are fortifications built in the reign of Henry VIII.

By 1997, EWS livery was starting to spread across the nation and No. 37415 is seen here in pristine condition on 15 May 1997 in the first version of the livery at Fratton with a charter from London Victoria, which had been steam hauled to Portsmouth with the steam locomotive running light to Portsmouth Harbour for the return working.

No. 221138 passes the container terminal at Redbridge in Southampton on 6 May 2013 with 1M54 13.45 Bournemouth–Manchester Piccadilly. As well as having an additional standard-class trailer, Class 221s also have a tilt mechanism for increased speeds, although the CrossCountry examples have all had their tilt equipment isolated to reduce costs and increase reliability.

No. 450557 breezes past Battledown flyover at Worting Junction on 13 April 2016 with 2B39 13.39 London Waterloo–Poole. This is one of three flyovers built by the Southern Railway to ease congestion, the others being at Pirbright Junction and Hampton Court Junction. Future plans are to add a similar structure at Woking.

Following several technical issues with Class 155 units, the decision was taken to create seventy single-car Class 153s from them. The new single-car units were allocated across the country with Cardiff Canton using theirs for local services in Wales and Bristol and for stopping services to Southampton. No. 153382 is seen here on 2 May 2000 at Eastleigh with the 16.02 Romsey–Worcester Shrub Hill.

No. 165119 arriving at Basingstoke on 10 November 2010 with 2J39 14.07 Reading–Basingstoke. Some of these units will be replaced soon with new electric stock, which is likely to see many of them head west and forge new ground on Portsmouth–Cardiff services, although they have already been mostly displaced by Class 150 stock on the Reading–Basingstoke shuttle service.

A large number of Class 150/2 units were delivered to Cardiff in the late 1980s for use on Valley Lines services and to supplement the longer distance Class 155 and then Class 158 units. Stopping services between Bristol and Southampton were a staple of the class and on 17 August 2000 No. 150238 was operating the 10.33 Bristol Temple Meads–Southampton Central, seen here approaching Southampton.

No. 66012 is seen in the spring sunshine just after passing Bedhampton station on 31 March 2016 with 7V07 12.41 Chichester–Merehead Quarry. This working runs once a week and is frequently hauled by a Class 59 as it threads its way past the Solent and on to Wiltshire.

Class 421 No. 1249 is seen here at Eastleigh on 2 April 1989 with a service from London Waterloo to Lymington Pier. The unit is sporting the first version of Network South East livery in which a selection of rolling stock was painted from 1986 onwards but, by summer 1988, it was revised using a darker shade of blue.

No. 158953 appears to have had a minor collision at some point, as part of the cowling has come off, and the snowplough would suggest this coach is part of one of the former ScotRail units that came south after the arrival of the Class 170 Turbostars in 1999. It's seen here passing Southampton Container Terminal on 6 June 2013 with a Cardiff service.

No. 43014 seen at Southampton Central at the rear of the 11.20 Bournemouth–Edinburgh Waverley on 15 January 2000. This locomotive is one of a small number of High Speed Train power cars that were fitted with standard buffer and coupling equipment for use as driving van trailers with Class 91s, prior to squadron introduction of Mark IV vehicles.

Class 442 No. 2403 passes Eastleigh on 4 March 1990 with a service from London Waterloo to Bournemouth. Less than two years since introduction, and already the panels that cover the jumper cables on either side of the cab have been removed. These panels are still missing on most units to this day.

No. 159008 at the head of a nine-coach formation of Class 159 units heading past Potbridge near Winchfield at speed in the autumn light on 10 November 2010 with 1L33 12.20 Waterloo–Exeter. This service splits at Salisbury with three coaches heading to Bristol, and three to Exeter, with the remaining three taken out of service.

For a while around 2012 to 2014, Eastleigh yard had a Class 60 acting as a 'Super Shunter' in addition to the regular Class 08 locomotive. No. 60074 in its unique but bright livery with DB Schenker branding is seen here on 8 April 2014, adjacent to the station and awaiting its next shunting duty.

No. 47839 is seen here disturbing the peace of the Somerstown area of Portsmouth as it starts the journey north with 1M32 14.14 Portsmouth & Southsea–Blackpool North on 7 March 2000 while displaying a pleasant mix of Virgin Trains and InterCity liveries, which were so common in the early days of the privatisation era.

Class 423 No. 3578 sweeps around the corner as it leaves Southampton Central station on 19 May 2001 with 1B11 08.45 London Waterloo–Poole. The livery is a variation of Network South East livery that was taken up as the standard livery of South West Trains for the fleet of slam-door stock in the 1990s.

Above: No. 159022 arrives at a very frosty Fareham station on 30 December 2000 with 1O31 09.54 Reading–Brighton. These services were supplemented with additional direct electric trains between Basingstoke and Brighton, so that there was an hourly fast service along the Sussex coast. However they were withdrawn in 2008 when Southern started operating additional services to Southampton.

Below: No. 450558 leaves Fratton on 22 October 2013 with 1P39 13.30 London Waterloo–Portsmouth. This unit was one of twenty-eight to be reclassified as Class 450/5 high-capacity units in 2007 for use on suburban services to Windsor, Weybridge and Hounslow but, in 2012, they returned to almost original condition and became part of the normal fleet.

No. 221139 passing Millbrook on 8 April 2014 with a service from Manchester Piccadilly to Bournemouth. The introduction of the Voyagers in September 2002 was dubbed 'Operation Princess' but issues with overcrowding and engineering teething troubles meant that a significant contraction of the network was agreed with the Strategic Rail Authority within months to improve the reliability of the services.

The recent development of re-engineered Class 73/9s has seen the class cover new ground, particularly on overnight sleeper services. However, the standard Class 73 still enjoys plenty of use on its traditional stomping ground across the Home Counties; No. 73138 is seen here at the rear of 1Q 53 13.50 Eastleigh at Worting Junction near Basingstoke on 18 April 2016.

Class 150/1 trains were the first production batch of 'Sprinter' units built to replace heritage stock in the 1980s. No. 150106 was one of many that were sent to work in the West Midlands but were displaced by Class 172s in 2012 before being transferred to Great Western. It is seen here passing Millbrook with a service from Southampton to Great Malvern on 18 April 2013.

Class 411 unit No. 1578 pauses at Eastleigh on a damp 26 January 2001 with 1Y28 11.00 Brighton–Basingstoke. The class was introduced in the late 1950s and had a full refurbishment at Swindon Works between 1979 and 1984. They were mostly based on primary routes in Kent but a few saw service in Hampshire in their latter years, prior to withdrawal in 2005.

No. 158881 disappears into Southampton tunnel on 7 July 2013 with a 'Romsey Rocket' service from Salisbury to Romsey. This first travels through Redbridge before arriving at Romsey via Eastleigh and the recently opened station at Chandlers Ford, which is one of very few single platform stations on the South West Trains network.

Class 421 No. 1308 leaving Southampton Central on 22 August 2000 with 1B31 13.45 London Waterloo–Poole, which was a semi-fast service with Brockenhurst being the next stop. This unit was one of twenty-two 'Greyhound' units that were modified for increased performance at higher speeds on the Portsmouth line with its steep gradients.

Storm clouds appear to be gathering in the distance over Reading but the sun still shines on No. 66556 as it powers away from a signal check in the Hampshire countryside and approaches Battledown flyover on 13 April 2016 with 4O49 09.22 Crewe Basford Hall–Southampton.

No. 450559 sits under the station lights at Portsmouth & Southsea on 27 November 2014, having just arrived with 2P63 19.45 London Waterloo–Portsmouth & Southsea. Only two of the original five low-level platforms remain in use, but it is common nowadays for more than one train to use each platform at once.

No. 159011 passes Old Basing with 1L35 12.50 Waterloo–Yeovil Pen Mill on 18 March 2016, while No. 159019 heads in the opposite direction with 1L42 12.47 Salisbury–Waterloo. The Yeovil Pen Mill service is a recent addition to the South West Trains network, which commenced with the 2015 winter timetable.

In 2003 No. 47290 was called to the Class 57 project and became No. 57316. After spending time at Virgin Trains followed by a short spell with Arriva Trains Wales, it moved to the West Coast Railway Company and is seen here taking the empty stock from a railtour into Fratton depot on 21 February 2015.

Above: Railtrack inherited a venerable fleet of various departmental trains, which were replaced by new multipurpose vehicles working in pairs, known as MPVs. The new trains were built in Germany and are a variation of short, fixed-formation freight trains used in Europe. Train DR98922 is pictured leaving Eastleigh on 10 October 2013.

Below: No. 43195 at Southampton Central at the rear of the 11.20 Bournemouth–Edinburgh Waverley on 6 November 1999, wearing what many consider to be the best livery these locomotives have carried. The InterCity 'Swallow' livery was introduced in 1987 and lasted well beyond privatisation, which for this power car meant being part of Virgin Trains.

No. 313205 arriving at Fratton on 9 July 2015 with 2N09 09.04 Brighton–Portsmouth Harbour. Class 313s began to operate in Hampshire in late 2010 replacing Class 377/3 units, which were required elsewhere. At the time of their introduction, there was widespread criticism of their use and in particular the lack of toilet facilities.

All of the Class 423 units based on the south-western division were allocated to Wimbledon as they were considered outer suburban stock, despite often working long-distance services. No. 3035 is seen here at Portsmouth Harbour in the fading light of a Sunday evening with the 21.20 Portsmouth Harbour–London Waterloo on 5 July 1992.

On a glorious summer day Class 442 No. 2419 heads in to Southampton Central on 22 July 2000 with 1W36 14.34 Wareham–London Waterloo. These units are still widely regarded as the best EMUs of the BR era and their 'snug' area by the buffet was unique when it was introduced and is still much missed.

Seen at Eastleigh on 7 May 2002, Class 411 No. 1563 has charge of 2B39 17.35 Eastleigh–Southampton Central. This unit was one of a batch of around thirty transferred to South West Trains in 1998 after a long career on services in Kent, due to a shortage of stock on SWT. Their time based at Fratton was reasonably short lived with final withdrawal taking place in 2004.

In May 1988 Class 155s were introduced on the Portsmouth–Cardiff route to replace Class 33 locomotives and, although they were an initial success, they eventually encountered sufficient technical problems for the class to be disbanded except for a small fleet in Yorkshire. Shortly before withdrawal No. 155321 is pictured here at Cosham with a Cardiff service on 13 May 1991.

No. 220032 passing Eastleigh on 10 October 2013 as it crosses the junction to the north of the station with 1O84 07.25 Newcastle–Southampton. Although the Voyagers don't yet have the character of the Class 47s they replaced, they are at least slightly more photogenic by having a sloped nose to catch as much light as possible.

Nos 377104 and 377111 meet as they pass Sydenham Terrace in Portsmouth on 2 June 2013 in a section of track that was once part of a canal traversing Portsmouth in the early nineteenth century, hence its somewhat sunken appearance. The canal bed became the route for the railway, which opened in 1847 linking Portsmouth and London.

Class 47s ruled the roost on CrossCountry services from the Dorset Coast from the early 1970s until the arrival of 'Virgin Voyagers' in 2002, although Class 43s supplemented the service in the 1990s. No. 47722 is seen here at Winchester with 1O09 08.17 Manchester–Bournemouth on 20 January 2001.

Class 421 No. 1908 approaches Southampton Central after a canter through the New Forest on a warm, summery 17 August 2000 with the 11.50 Bournemouth–London Victoria. This particular unit was one of a handful to receive the new livery of Southern Railway when Govia took over the Connex South Central Franchise in 2001.

On the cold and icy morning of 30 December 2000, No. 158869 pauses at Cosham with 1F05 07.30 Cardiff Central–Portsmouth Harbour. This class member was one of the last batch of units to be produced and came with more powerful engines than the earlier examples, resulting in increased acceleration.

Above: No. 450569 traverses the level crossing after leaving Havant on 31 March 2016 with 5Y00 10.15 Southampton–Woking, which runs purely to retain route knowledge of the Guildford line for Bournemouth crew. This unit was delivered as No. 450069 and became No. 450569 when modified for inner suburban use; despite its return to the mainline fleet, the number remains.

Below: On 5 June 2013 No. 444024 passes Millbrook Container Terminal with 2B52 13.50 Poole–London Waterloo stopping service. This transfer point is used for containers being delivered by road with the much larger terminal about a mile to the west at Redbridge for freight heading in and out by sea.

Class 456s were introduced in 1990 to replace Class 416 stock on routes from Victoria, and just over twenty years later they moved to South West Trains and are currently the booked traction on the Ascot–Guildford line. No. 456004 is pictured leaving Aldershot on 9 June 2016 with 2N36 12.00 Guildford–Ascot.

Freightliner have a crew depot at Eastleigh station so the majority of their services make a stop to change driver in the platform. It is therefore reasonably uncommon to see a Freightliner service running through on the Down fast line, which is exactly what No. 66533 was doing on 10 October 2013.